THE HARRY BOOK

totally
written & illustrated by
absolutely

Cheryl Harness

"He was the kind of president the founding fathers
had in mind for the country. He came directly from
the people. He *was* America."
David McCullough, historian

Library of Congress Control Number: 2008911823
ISBN: 978-0-9822920-0-6

A Note from the Author

We know that he was from Missouri and that he unleashed a horrific weapon only weeks after the burdens of the wartime presidency fell on his shoulders. What else should we know about Harry Truman? Know that he was a dutiful son, a farmer, and a respected leader of men in battle. Some of the people with whom he associated had shady reputations, but Harry was an honest man, loyal to his much-loved wife and to his friends. Despite his lack of a college degree, he was an educated man, thanks to years of serious reading. He was a plain-talking lover of music, architecture, and literature. He was passionate student of history, too. "You'll notice if you read your history," Harry said once, "that the work of the world gets done by people who aren't bellyachers." Harry was no bellyacher.

A note on the text: Much of what is said by Harry and others in his life, I paraphrase for the sake of space and clarity. These words and specific quotations are taken from President Truman's memoirs and books noted in the bibliography.

Back in the 1960s, I used to walk past Harry's big white house on Delaware Street on my way to school, but I only saw him once, and then from afar, when he was speaking to a crowd up at his Library. The hot sun glinted on his glasses. Over the years I've been asked more than once when I was going to write about him, seeing as we claim the same hometown. Had I known that writing and illustrating this book was going to be so much fun, I'd never have waited so long.

C.H., 2008
Independence, Missouri
Queen City of the Trails

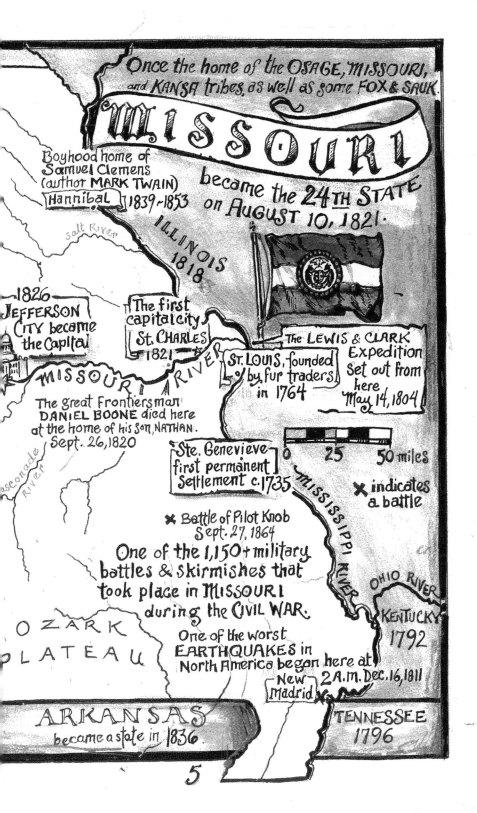

Once the home of the OSAGE, MISSOURI, and KANSA tribes, as well as some FOX & SAUK

MISSOURI

became the 24TH STATE on AUGUST 10, 1821.

Boyhood home of Samuel Clemens (author MARK TWAIN)
Hannibal 1839-1853

ILLINOIS 1818

salt River

1826 JEFFERSON CITY became the Capital

The first capital city St. CHARLES 1821

MISSOURI RIVER

St. LOUIS, founded by fur traders in 1764

The LEWIS & CLARK Expedition set out from here May 14, 1804

The great Frontiersman DANIEL BOONE died here at the home of his son, NATHAN. Sept. 26, 1820

Gasconade River

Ste. Genevieve first permanent settlement c. 1735

0   25   50 miles

✗ indicates a battle

✗ Battle of Pilot Knob Sept. 27, 1864
One of the 1,150+ military battles & skirmishes that took place in MISSOURI during the CIVIL WAR.

MISSISSIPPI RIVER

OHIO RIVER

KENTUCKY 1792

OZARK PLATEAU

One of the worst EARTHQUAKES in North America began here at 2 A.M. Dec. 16, 1811
New Madrid ✗

ARKANSAS became a state in 1836.

TENNESSEE 1796

5

Both sets of my grandparents left Shelby County, KENTUCKY, in the 1840s and went to MISSOURI.

MISSOURI RIVER · MISSISSIPPI RIVER · OHIO RIVER

LOUISA YOUNG and her husband, SOLOMON.

Our daughter Mattie will be Harry's mama.

ANDERSON SHIPPE TRUMAN and his wife MARY JANE

Our boy John will be Harry's papa.

My wagon trains went out to CALIFORNIA and back.

With the help of their slaves, the YOUNGS and the TRUMANS established farms in Jackson County, MISSOURI, down by Grandview. Harry's Grandpa YOUNG was a wagon master, too.

Pulled by a dozen oxen or maybe that many mules, "He'd have a huge wagon a huge wagon that could haul tons of freight...as many as 24 or 30 of them in a train." · HST ·

Martha Ellen "Mattie" Young born Nov. 25, 1852

When my parents were small, THE HOT question—whether or not legal slavery would spread west—flared into BORDER WAR

John Anderson Truman born Dec. 5, 1851

Armed men burned farms, towns; stole, killed, and terrified people on both sides of the state line.

LAWRENCE KANSAS "FREE" STATE Jan. 29, 1861

Vernon Osceola Bates Cass Jackson County

MISSOURI

1855~1865

* LOUISA YOUNG & MATTIE at Grandview Farm

Pro-UNION KANSAS "Jayhawkers" loot & burn Osceola, MO.

1861

Pro-Confederate "bushwhackers" from MISSOURI raid Lawrence, KS. 150 men & boys are killed.

1863

Blue-coated Union soldiers came to SOLOMON Young's Farm.

"They killed our hogs & stole everything that was loose!"

To punish MISSOURIANS after the raid on Lawrence, KS, and to keep them from aiding the enemy., Union Gen. THOS. EWING issued ORDER No. 11 to rural folks in Jackson, Cass, Bates, & Vernon Counties: they had but 15 days to evacuate their farms.

Then Federal troops set fire to their houses. The BORDER WAR scarred up the land & the people, too.

"When I was six, Vivian three, and Mary one year old, we moved to INDEPENDENCE"

That was in 1890 —

65 years after the Osage gave up their MISSOURI lands and white settlers came to this hilly place known for its clear springs.

60 years or so after INDEPENDENCE became the eastern end of the MERCHANTS' trail to SANTA FE.

57 years after Joseph Smith's followers were tormented and run out of town.

49 years after the first of many wagon trains set out on the emigrants' trail to the OREGON COUNTRY.

At first we lived at 619 South CRYSLER. Then, when I was about 12, we moved to another fine big house at 909 west WALDO.

41 years after legions of "49-ers" came rushing through town on their way to CALIFORNIA GOLD.

30 years after Joseph Smith's son reorganized the "Saints" into the church now known as the Community of CHRIST, headquartered here.

20+ years after the CIVIL WAR began hereabouts, on the bloody BORDER

HARRY S. TRUMAN will bring even more significance to his HISTORIC HOMETOWN.

North Crysler Avenue

NETTLETON

W. COLLEC

W. WALDO

WHITE OAK

TRUMAN formerly VAN HORN Rd and/or BLUE AVE.

FLOURNOY HOUSE built in 1826!

ELM

Train Station

CRYSLER

TRUMANS' HOME 1890-1896

South

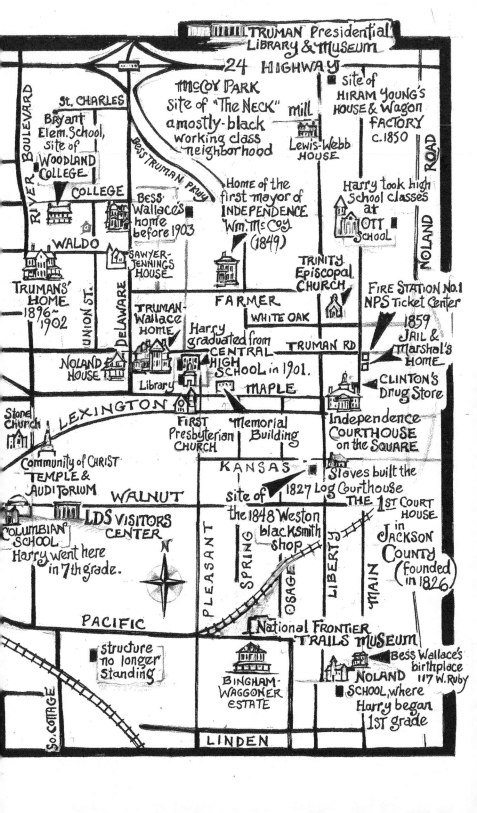

"So I got a job as a time-keeper at a railroad construction outfit."

Some 8 or 10 months later, I went to work for the KANSAS CITY *Star.*

$9 a week — a raise in pay!

Early in 1903 or late in 1902 I went to work at the NATIONAL BANK of COMMERCE at 10TH & Walnut in KANSAS CITY as a clerk at $35 a month.

In 1905 I went to work for the UNION NATIONAL BANK for $75 a month.

HARRY divided his pay between his family's bills, rent at his boarding house, streetcar fare, & cheap seats at the ORPHEUM Theatre 9th & May or the SHUBERT THEATRE 104 W. 10th

Sometimes I stopped by Jesse James, Jr.'s SODA FOUNTAIN & CANDY SHOP.

An ice cream soda, please.

That'll be 5¢

OR TALBOT'S *Hippodrome* OR THE *Grand Opera* HOUSE

14

President Teddy ROOSEVELT made a speech in K.C., down at 10th & Main.

"He had a very high tenor voice & it carried very well. [Everybody] wanted to see him grin & show his teeth, which he did... The Roosevelts were none of them very big people & they all seemed to have a lot of teeth to show." HST

From my reading about world history & government, I decided that every citizen should know something about military, finance or banking, & agriculture.

"Harry, this is the first time since 1863 that a blue uniform has been in this house. Don't bring it here again."

He didn't!

Harry went out to the Grandview farm to show Grandmother YOUNG his new blue uniform. She didn't like it!

So I started my military education by joining the MISSOURI National Guard. June 14, 1905

In the year 1906, my family needed me back on the farm.

15

The GREAT WAR, later known as WORLD WAR I, broke out in AUGUST 1914. It quickly turned into a nightmare of death & destruction.

ALLIES (more than 20 nations, ultimately)
CENTRAL POWERS
NEUTRAL

"The world must be made safe for democracy."

U.S. President WOODROW WILSON

GERMAN Submarine warfare pushed the U.S. into the War on the side of the ALLIES APRIL 6, 1917

Patriotic, 33-year-old Harry rejoined the NATIONAL GUARD. (He'd dropped out in 1911.) He helped organize the 2ND MO. Field Artillery Battery. It became the 129TH FIELD ARTILLERY, a regiment attached to the 35TH DIVISION of the U.S. ARMY.

Harry memorized the eye chart so he could pass the ARMY Physical!

Let's be married before you go over-seas!

No — you musn't tie yourself to a man who could come home a cripple. Or not at all. We'll be married, Bess, when I come home.

And he left me & Mamma to run the farm. We did OUR patriotic duty OVER HERE!

I was determined to do my duty over there.*

VIVIAN

* the title of George M. COHAN'S BIG HIT song of the day.

"I'll never forget how my love cried on my shoulder when I told her I was going. That was worth a lifetime on this earth." HST

20

*men's "furnishings" (accessories)

Hot-headed MIKE PENDERGAST (Jim's father, Harry's mentor)

Everyone knew that HARRY was okay. An honest man, fine WAR record & a good family. A MASON, a BAPTIST & an American Legionnaire.

In 1922, I ran for JUDGE of the County's eastern district— an administrative job. No black robes. I licked the other 4 candidates. I had more friends & kinfolks than they did!

"We have the theory that if we do a man a favor he will do us one."

Thos. J. "BIG TOM" Pendergast a.k.a. The BOSS

(Alderman Jim's younger brother)

Generous, high-living, high-rolling Big TOM P. ran saloons, concrete & construction businesses, & his political organization with MASTERY, bribery, & Violence. in a time (1920s & 30s) & place (KC) of gangsters & jazz. Friendly, honorable HARRY brought the corrupt machine some respectability. His enemies will taunt him with the name of Thos. J.

PENDERGAST

Harry's & Bess's only child was born on February 17, 1924 in the big house at 219 North DELAWARE. She'd grow up there with her parents & grandmother, Madge Wallace

MARY MARGARET TRUMAN

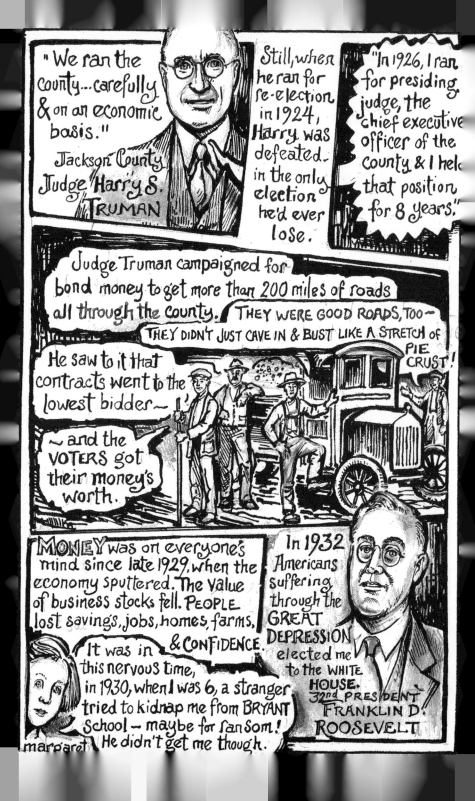

"I pledge you, I pledge myself to a new deal for the American people." Franklin D. Roosevelt 1932

AS PRESIDING JUDGE OF JACKSON COUNTY, Harry was responsible for an annual budget of $7 million & 700 employees & 2 county courthouses & jails.

The new county courthouse in KC was dedicated in Dec. 1934. By then Harry was on his way to Washington.

*

One of the proudest days of my life was that day in Sept. 1933 when we dedicated our remodeled expanded courthouse here in Independence.

TRUMAN U.S. SENATOR

A NEW DEAL FOR MISSOURI

VOTE FOR TRUMAN!

"In 19&34 I was finished with the county; I'd done my job..." HST

* Harry chose Charles Keck to sculpt the courthouse statue of Gen. Andrew Jackson.

27

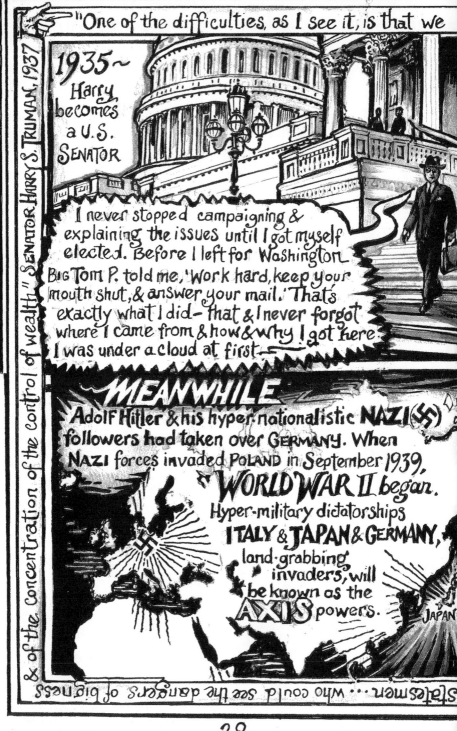

"SENATOR HARRY S. TRUMAN, 1937"

1935~ Harry becomes a U.S. SENATOR

I never stopped campaigning & explaining the issues until I got myself elected. Before I left for Washington, Big Tom P. told me, 'Work hard, keep your mouth shut, & answer your mail.' That's exactly what I did—that & I never forgot where I came from & how & why I got here. I was under a cloud at first—

MEANWHILE

Adolf Hitler & his hyper-nationalistic **NAZI** followers had taken over GERMANY. When NAZI forces invaded POLAND in September 1939, **WORLD WAR II** began. Hyper-military dictatorships **ITALY & JAPAN & GERMANY,** land-grabbing invaders, will be known as the **AXIS** powers.

JAPAN

& of the concentration of the control of wealth"

HARRY reported his findings to President ROOSEVELT & to the SENATE in early, 1941: Defense contractors were using the WAR to cheat the government & waste the taxpayers' money. The Senate formed the COMMITTEE to INVESTIGATE the NATIONAL DEFENSE PROGRAM.

It came to be known as the TRUMAN COMMITTEE as HARRY was its chairman. It speeded war production on the homefront, saving the government some $15 BILLION AND the committee may well have saved the lives of U.S. sailors, soldiers, & marines.

We traveled all over the country watchdogging the War effort, then I conducted many a public hearing here at the CAPITOL.

IN THE HARD, WORRISOME WORLD WAR II YEARS, HARRY'S FELLOW LAWMAKERS & THOUSANDS OF AMERICANS CAME TO ADMIRE THE GENIAL, DETERMINED, NO-NONSENSE SENATOR FROM MISSOURI. THEN, in 1944~

Great Britain
LONDON ★
Netherlands
Belgium
LUX.
Rhine River
PARIS
France
JUNE 6 D-DAY

BERLIN
NAZI Germany

Gen. Dwight D. Eisenhower directs the long-awaited Allied invasion of NAZI-occupied Western EUROPE.

August 18

HST & FDR meet at the White House for lunch...

sharp & complex mind

pale & haggard
strained ♡ heart

JULY 21 DEMOCRATIC NATIONAL CONVENTION ~ a hot night in CHICAGO, ILLINOIS~

Bess
Margaret
TRUMAN
We didn't want this job.
Pa's won the vice presidential nomination! *

trembling hands

* FDR's 3rd-term VP Henry A. Wallace got dumped from the ticket.

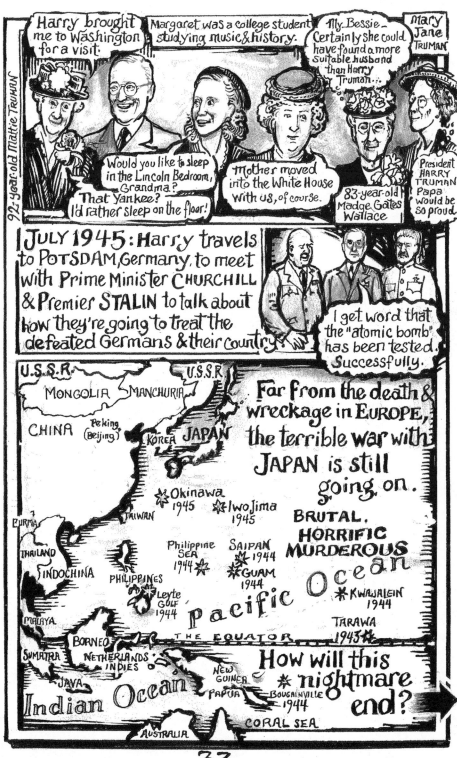

33

So long WWII. Hello COLD WAR

An INTENSE rivalry between the democratic nations of the WEST & the communist-controlled countries of the EAST

A 45-year-long war of nerves between the U.S. & the UNION of SOVIET SOCIALIST REPUBLICS

Baltic Sea

Moscow

IRON Curtain

Berlin · Stettin (Szczecin)
East Germany
West Germany
France
Switz.
Austria
Trieste
Italy
Poland
Czechoslovakia
Hungary
Yugoslavia
Adriatic Sea
Albania
Romania
Bulgaria
GREECE
Black Sea

USSR Flag: MOSTLY RED, get it? "RED" COMMUNIST.

"From Stettin in the Baltic to Trieste in the Adriatic an iron curtain has descended across the [European] Continent."
Winston Churchill at Fulton, Missouri (Harry invited him.)
March 5, 1946

Premier JOSEPH STALIN, cruel dictator of the U.S.S.R. a.k.a. the SOVIET UNION a.k.a. communist RUSSIA. After WWII the U.S.S.R. takes strict control over its part of DEFEATED DIVIDED GERMANY. BY 1948, the rest of Eastern EUROPE were Soviet-run police states, isolated behind an imaginary "iron curtain."

COULD THE WORLD BE SAVED FROM RED DOMINATION? (maybe, with some help from the U.S....)

"I believe that we must assist free peoples to work out their destinies in their own way." HST in a speech to the CONGRESS March 12, 1947

the "TRUMAN" DOCTRINE

March 16, 1947

Margaret Truman

I made my singing debut with the symphony in Detroit, MICHIGAN!

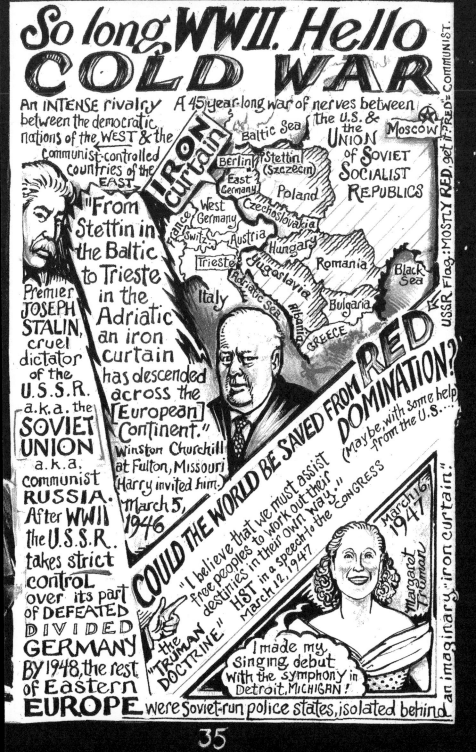

35

1948
A Year in the LIFE of PRESIDENT HARRY S. TRUMAN

· January ·

"We have learned that a healthy world economy is essential to world peace."

HST delivers his 3rd State of the Union Address

· February ·

HST calls for civil rights laws, an end to the crime of lynching, & to racial discrimination.

I WENT ON A TRIP TO KEY WEST, FLORIDA (to my Little White House) & ON TO CUBA & PUERTO RICO.

· March ·

Not everyone liked Harry's idea — at first

The WHITE HOUSE gets its "TRUMAN BALCONY."

· April ·

The U.S. begins sending billions of dollars to wrecked & starving EUROPE to help it recover from WWII. This MARSHALL PLAN was proposed by the great ex-General, HST's Secretary of State GEORGE C. MARSHALL

As a bonus, this critical foreign aid will keep Europe from falling under SOVIET control.

· May ·

Harry's old haberdasher friend, Eddie Jacobson, a JEW, implores Harry to support U.S. recognition of the new state of ISRAEL. (HST did indeed.)

° June °

After the SOVIETS "SEAL OFF" BERLIN to all trucks, cars, & trains, HST orders the **BERLIN AIRLIFT.**
For 320 days, planes deliver coal, food ~ even candy ~ to blockaded BERLINERS until the U.S.S.R. finally gives in.

French / British ➔ East Berlin (soviet)
U.S. ➔ West Berlin

Hamburg / British Zone / BERLIN / EAST GERMANY (soviet)

WEST GERMANY

Bonn / Frankfurt / U.S. Zone / French Zones ➔ / Munich

Enlarged view of divided BERLIN
(Not until 1990 will Germany & its capital city be reunited.)

YIKES!

° July °

We'll beat those REPUBLICANS * & make 'em like it!

A hot night in PHILADELPHIA, PA ~ HST becomes the DEMOCRATS' presidential candidate in his own right.

HST issues an EXECUTIVE ORDER: The U.S. ARMED FORCES are no longer to be SEGREGATED

° August °
In the nearly-150-year-old White House, in Margaret's sitting room, the floor caves in!

° September °
HST formally opens his campaign DETROIT, Michigan

° September • October °
33 days • 21,928 miles

"You get a real feeling of this country & the people in it when you're on a train, speaking from the back of a train." HST

THE WHISTLE-STOP CAMPAIGN

I'm not asking you to vote for me. Vote for yourselves. If you want to live like a Republican, you'd better vote like a Democrat!

GIVE 'EM HELL, HARRY!

November HA HA HA!

Chicago Tribune DEWEY DEFEATS TRUMAN

WOW! HARRY WON!

° December °
Still, the TRUMANS had to leave the WHITE HOUSE ~ it wasn't safe!

* Actually, hardly anyone but Harry thought that Harry could defeat his Republican opponent, Thomas E. DEWEY.

pop & the drapes move back & forth. I can just imagine old

"The floors

An abandoned hotel — that's what the White House was like when we moved in. Cracked plaster, swaying, sagging floors. The chandeliers trembled over our heads.

Oh my, the way the old place creaked & groaned, a man might well think that the White House was haunted!

George Washington himself oversaw the design of this House in 1792. Nothing but its brick & sandstone walls were left after the British burned the place in 1814. It had been rebuilt then remodled, renovated, & lived in hard. Now, in 1948, its wooden beams were so weakened, the WHITE HOUSE was dangerously close to COLLAPSE!

+ BLAIR HOUSE +

THE PRESIDENTS' GUEST HOUSE.

We built a steel skeleton inside these old stone walls.

Under them will be a deep, strong concrete foundation—

And a 2-story basement

a bomb shelter too

"I consider history—our history—to be

38

While all the work was going on, we lived in BLAIR HOUSE, across Pennsylvania Avenue from the White House. Dad loved history AND architecture so he went over to inspect the construction every chance he got.

The naked walls of the WHITE HOUSE revealed the marks of stoneworkers' chisels from the 1790s.

This house stands for the story of the UNITED STATES. Its reconstruction took more than 3 years & cost almost $6 million: a lot of money, trouble, & worry, but it was worth it.

Dining Room

Entrance Hall

State Dining Room

Red Room

Blue Room

Green Room

East Room

HST

South Portico

When the work was done, in 1952, I gave the American people a televised tour of their Presidents' HOUSE.

"I pray Heaven to bestow the best of blessings on this House & on all that shall hereafter inhabit it. May none but honest & wise men ever rule under this roof." President JOHN ADAMS, 1800

Franklin D. Roosevelt ... "This place is haunted sure as shootin'." ... HST ... John F. Kennedy 35th President.

brutal, destructive

The KOREAN WAR

began on June 25, 1950.

SOVIET UNION a.k.a.

COMMUNIST forces led by MAO ZEDONG are taking over CHINA (1946~1949)

NORTH KOREA

PYONGYANG

SEOUL

Sea of JAPAN

YELLOW SEA

SOUTH KOREA

JAPAN

the UNION of SOVIET SOCIALIST REPUBLICS (U.S.S.R.) or the communist RUSSIAN Empire

Communist forces from NORTH KOREA INVADED South KOREA.

"If this was allowed to go unchallenged it would mean a "third world war." HST

Sending U.S. troops to help defend SOUTH KOREA was the toughest decision of my political career.

Before the fighting ends in JULY 1953 more than 2 million UN, Chinese, & Korean troops are killed, wounded, or taken prisoner.

I thought we should have bombed red CHINA after they got into the war.

5-STAR General DOUGLAS MacARTHUR publicly disagreed with HARRY on how he was running the WAR in KOREA.

April 1951

That brass hat prima donna disrespected the office of the PRESIDENCY so I FIRED him — stirred up quite a stink!

Princess Elizabeth & Prince Philip of GREAT BRITAIN came to call on the TRUMANS in October 1951.

Mrs. TRUMAN & I moved back into the redone WHITE HOUSE on March 27, 1952.

STILL, I'd much prefer to live in INDEPENDENCE!

"I shall not be a candidate for reelection." HST March 29, 1952

I won the 1952 election, & became the 34TH PRESIDENT on Jan. 20, 1953.

Former General DWIGHT D. EISENHOWER

Then MR. & MRS. TRUMAN went home to MISSOURI.

HARRY S. TRUMAN, Independence, Missouri

Harry took his morning walks in his old neighborhood & he had a happy day at his daughter's wedding.

Clifton Daniel & Margaret Truman

April 21, 1956

BESS   HARRY

Harry's friends & a bunch of Independence boosters raised the money & set aside land for the

HARRY S. TRUMAN LIBRARY & MUSEUM

A fine place for my papers, for me to work on my MEMOIRS, & for the CITIZENS to learn about the PRESIDENCY.

My husband Franklin created the 1st presidential library near our home at HYDE PARK NEW YORK.

ELEANOR ROOSEVELT & Ex-President HERBERT HOOVER were among those who came to the DEDICATION on JULY 6, 1957.

Over the next years, Harry Truman's fellow PRESIDENTS came to visit him & his library.

Mrs. Kennedy & I invited President & Mrs. TRUMAN back to the WHITE HOUSE in 1961 for a return visit.

The people voted for HARRY TRUMAN not beca[use] he gave them hell—but because he gave them hope.

Presiden[t] Eisenho[wer] came to t[he] TRUMAN LIBRAR[Y] too, in Novembe[r] 1961.

President LYNDON B. JOHNSON came to INDEPENDENCE to sign the MEDICARE BILL in 1965—20 years after President TRUMAN began pushing for health care legislation.

President RICHARD NIXON

President Nixon played the piano for me in 1969, when he came to visit—The Missouri Waltz—not my favorite tune Not my favorite president either—

In 1964, a bad slip & fall put Harry in the hospital & slowed him down. By 1972, his stomach & lungs were in dreadful shape.

I was a sick old man in the hospital over in Kansas City when I died on December 26, 1972. 88 years old! I was buried in the courtyard of my library. Nearly ten years passed before Bess died & my 97-year-old sweetheart was laid to rest beside me.

CHRONOLOGY

1884   Harry S. Truman is born in Lamar, MO, on May 8.

1900   Harry serves as a page at the Democratic National Convention in KCMO. (The Dems nominate William Jennings Bryan.)

1901-05   Harry works at the KC Star, the Santa Fe RR, the National Bank of Commerce then the Union National Bank in KCMO.

1905-11   HST serves in the Missouri National Guard.

1906   He moves to his family's farm in Grandview, MO.

1914   John Truman, Harry's father, dies on Nov. 2.

1917-19   HST serves as an artillery captain in France, in WWI.

1919   Harry Truman & Bess Wallace are married, June 28. HST & Eddie Jacobson open their haberdashery, Nov. 29.

1920   HST becomes a major in the Officers Reserve Corps.

1922   The haberdashery fails. With the help of the Pendergasts, HST enters politics & is elected Jackson County Eastern Judge.

1924   Mary Margaret Truman is born, Feb. 17.

1923-25   Harry attends night classes at the Kansas City School of Law.

1926   HST is elected Jackson County Presiding Judge, Nov. 2.

1934   HST is elected to the U.S. Senate, Nov. 6.

1941   Harry heads a Senate committee, investigating defense programs, critically important work as the US enters WWII after Japanese forces attack Pearl Harbor, Hawaii, Dec. 7.

1944   Harry is elected as President F. D. Roosevelt's VP, Nov. 7.

1945   FDR dies; HST becomes the 33rd President, April 12. • Germany surrenders, May 8 (VE Day). • Atomic bombs are dropped on Hiroshima, Aug. 6, then Nagasaki, Aug. 9. • Japan surrenders. Aug. 14 (VJ Day). • HST meets with Britain's Prime Minister Winston Churchill & Russian Premier Joseph Stalin at Potsdam, Germany, July 17~Aug.2. • The United Nations (UN) is founded, Oct. 24. • HST proposes a national health care program, Nov. 19.

1946   Winston Churchill delivers "Iron Curtain" speech at Fulton, MO, Mar. 5. The Cold War is beginning.

1949   Martha Young Truman, Harry's mother, dies, July 26.

1950-53   The Korean War is a major Cold War challenge to the UN.

1953   Dwight D. Eisenhower becomes the 34th President, Jan. 20. The Trumans return to Independence, MO.

1957   The Harry S. Truman Library & Museum is dedicated at Independence, MO, July 6.

1972   Harry S. Truman, 88, passes away, Dec. 26.

1982   Bess Wallace Truman, 97, dies on Oct. 18.

2008   Their daughter, Margaret Truman Daniel, 83, dies on Jan. 29.

Places Well Worth Visiting

• **Harry S. Truman Library and Museum**
500 West Highway 24, Independence, MO 64050
816.268.8200 or 800.833.1225
www.trumanlibrary.org

• **Harry S. Truman National Historic Site**
If you wish to tour Harry's and Bess's big white house at
219 North Delaware Street, in Independence, MO, or the
Truman Farm at 12301 Blue Ridge Boulevard, in Grandview,
MO, write or stop by the Visitors' Center at 223 North Main
Street, Independence, MO 64050 816.254.9929
www.nps.gov/hstr

• Find out about the war that changed HST's world forever at the
National World War I Museum, at the Liberty Memorial.
Harry was proud to take part in its 1921 dedication.
100 West 26th Street, Kansas City, MO 64108 816.784.1918
www.theworldwar.org/s/110/index.aspx

• For even more info on the place where Harry came of age,
visit the Jackson County Historical Society at www.jchs.org
and learn about the truly historic courthouse on the
Independence Square, where Harry used to work:
http://trumancourthouse.org/default.aspx

• For all kinds of extra, excellent information, check out these
websites:
www.ci.independence.mo.us
www.whitehouse.gov/history/presidents
www.visitmo.com
www.indepmo.org

**"I'm not sure he was right about the atomic bomb or even Korea,
but remembering him reminds people what a man in that office ought to be
like. It's character, just character. He stands like a rock in memory now."**
Eric Sevareid, journalist

Bibliography

Ferrell, Robert H., Editor. *The Autobiography of Harry S. Truman*. Niwot, CO: University Press of Colorado, 1980.

Hamby, Alonzo L. *Man of the People*. New York: Oxford University Press, 1995.

Lazo, Caroline Evensen. *Harry S. Truman*. Minneapolis, MN: Lerner Publications Co., 2003.

McCullough, David. *Truman*. New York: Touchstone/Simon & Schuster, 1992.

Miller, Merle. *Plain Speaking, An oral biography of Harry S. Truman*. NY: Berkley Publishing Corp., 1974.

Taylor, Jon E. *A President, a Church, and Trails West*. Columbia, MO: University of Missouri Press, 2008.

Acknowledgments

For their help and inspiration, I offer my thanks to William Anderson, Sharon Snyder, Veda Boyd Jones, to the folks at the HST Library & Museum, and most particularly, to the staff at the Mid-Continent Public Library, North Independence Branch.

About the Author

Cheryl Harness graduated from the University of Central Missouri in 1973 with an art education degree. Before becoming an author/illustrator, she spent her early working life as a greeting card artist. Since 1987, Cheryl has made countless school visits, talking to students about researching, writing, and illustrating her many historical picture books, such as *Ghosts of the White House, The Revolutionary John Adams,* and *Remember the Ladies: 100 Great American Women.* Information about these and other titles can be found at www.cherylharness.com. By the way, in *Just For You to Know.* Cheryl's novel set in 1963 Independence, Harry Truman makes a brief appearance.